get well

The Penguin Leunig

The Second Leunig

The Bedtime Leunig

A Bag of Roosters

Ramming the Shears

The Travelling Leunig

A Common Prayer

The Prayer Tree

Common Prayer Collection

Introspective

A Common Philosophy

Everyday Devils and Angels

A Bunch of Poesy

You and Me

Short Notes From the Long History of Happiness

Why Dogs Sniff Each Other's Tails

Goat person

The Curly Pyjama Letters

The Stick

Poems 1972–2002

Strange Creature

When I Talk to You

Wild Figments

A New Penguin Leunig

Hot

The Lot

The Essential Leunig

Holy Fool

Musings From the Inner Duck

The Wayward Leunig

Ducks for Dark Times

get well

Michael Leunig

PENGUIN BOOKS

PENGUIN BOOKS

UK | USA | Canada | Ireland | Australia
India | New Zealand | South Africa | China

Penguin Books is part of the Penguin Random House group of companies
whose addresses can be found at global.penguinrandomhouse.com.

Penguin
Random House
Australia

First published by Penguin Random House Pty Ltd, 2021

Cover illustration by Michael Leunig
Cover design by Michael Leunig © Penguin Random House Australia Pty Ltd
Typeset by Adam Laszczuk, Penguin Random House Australia Pty Ltd

Printed and bound in Singapore by COS.

NATIONAL
LIBRARY
OF AUSTRALIA
A catalogue record for this
book is available from the
National Library of Australia

ISBN 978 1 76104 489 2

penguin.com.au

A Note from the Author

It is said that most of the world's great work is done by people who are feeling just a little bit unwell. This is a heartening idea for a newspaper cartoonist like myself, who in more than fifty years has faced too many deadlines feeling a bit off-colour, slightly dreadful and a little too weary. The thought that it may be possible to create something unique, wise and funny while feeling poorly is worth clinging to as the publishing deadline looms.

Yet at some point in my working life I started to see that feelings of wretchedness and spiritual fragility could actually produce some very original and wonderful works. I began to understand that the struggle to create a lovely thing could lead to feelings of being so lost, hopeless and demoralised that it was crushing to the ego and to any hope of a confident, experienced self who knew what he was doing. Instead of making progress with the work in hand, I would frequently experience a most alarming internal regression.

So there I would find myself facing a deadline with all my creative faculties having deserted me, feeling more like a lost and lonely child than an editorial cartoonist – a vulnerable innocent, a hopeless fool in a panic – surrounded by a world of clever critics and brilliant, award-winning masterminds of the media. In my heart I was simply not up to the task of working in such a witty and dazzling environment.

And yet, and yet . . . in retrospect, and through experience, I was able to see that in these disturbing moments of loss and not knowing, my ego and all the worldliness that went with it had been reduced more or less to rubble, and that this humbling mess was in fact an achievement or a gift from the creativity gods that would allow me liberation, nonchalance and bravado enough to transcend the all-pervasive cult of cleverness and modern cynicism – and to create a more primal, personal and uninhibited world for a few hours in which I was free to experiment and play and discover and be sensitised according to my deepest, most personal loves and joys. What was there to lose now that I was so happily lost and carefree in my creativity? On a good day it almost became a state of rapture; a creative wellness that arose magically from the pain of surrendering to sensations of doubt, being poor of spirit and feeling unwell with the world. The creative heart just has to be brave and reckless, and learn to welcome the humbling or humiliating collapse of the ego – which indeed can often be the in-built enemy of art and truth. I also got to know that this long-suffering ego would come back refreshed, wiser and more mature when it was needed.

So here in this book are some of the cartoons I found during my struggles to the deadline in recent years; years marked for me by a serious head injury, a major domestic sadness and a potentially lethal cancer with the trauma of its associated radical surgery. Then just as I was beginning to heal, the world around me sank suddenly into darkness and dread as news of a viral pandemic swept headlong into the human spirit, limiting freedom, repressing humour and spreading a deep, divisive suspicion in my society. On some days the world seemed too emotionally unwell for the sublime ambiguities of cartooning; too grimly obsessed with data and death to tolerate the nourishing spiritual mysteries drawn simply with pen and ink. It was not easy for me to work.

Perhaps the cartoons gathered here in this collection may seem too infantile, sentimental or preachy for a harsh, humourless and unfriendly world – a fearful, censorious world of irritation, strident ideology and the desperate worship of cold science – but many of these pieces are what came to me most surely, naturally and sincerely during this strange period of creative exile from what seemed to be an increasingly stern and unforgiving environment. They could well be my acts of defiance against a perceived mad world that would shame and strip away our personal and peculiar innocence – which indeed is our birthright and the source of all genius and human beauty.

Many of the pieces hark back in temperament to my frugal childhood when my mother and grandmothers recited sentimental rhyming verses and my father offered funny, blunt aphorisms about life and death at the dinner table. And there were many sentimental songs as well, which have nourished my drawings over the years. All of these early pleasures went in deep like a type of emotional dialect or mother tongue – a sensual lingo full of yearning, joy, humour, wonder, sadness and sanity. That was the soulful sort of thing I often regressed to and found amongst the rubble after the creative ambition of the ego had collapsed during the searing struggle to a deadline; that's what remained intact and faithful – a sentiment that had survived within me after all those years – despite the wear and tear of art fashions and the critical atmosphere of urban culture where I had worked.

Yet when all is said and done, my cartoons remind me that if we can sometimes accept the collapse of our ambitions and hopes and allow ourselves to regress for a while, and in good faith dare to play in the rubble of our lives, and there in these ruins create images, words, art, relationships or loving humour, then indeed things may get well and be sane in ways that we could never have hoped for or imagined.

And what is wellness anyway? We can't get it and have it for keeps. Wellness is a bit like gardening or washing the dishes – you just have to keep doing it every day, for yourself and for your world.

FOR NOW

Get well
Do good
Make love
Touch wood
Be kind
Be true
Get well
Be you

PRAYER TO SELF

Gently swing from vine to vine,
Live from day to day,
Turning water into wine,
Loving what you may.

Learn to care and not to care,
Learn how not to know,
Feel your way from here to there,
Let it come and go.

Leunig

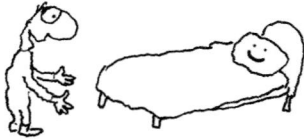

HYMN

Care is the cure.
It is slow,
It is raw,
It is pure.

It is simple and bare.
It is real,
It is bold,
It is there.

Nothing is newer
Or older,
Or wiser,
Or truer.
Care is the cure.

Leunig

Leunig

GOING TO SLEEP

Now I lay me down to sleep
With fragments drifting from
the deep;
The mysteries, the love and strife,
The wild creature that is life;
This life I do not understand,
The grieving heart, the open hand,
A careful step, a joyful leap,
The dream before we go to sleep,
The crazy world, a simple breath,
The life before we go to death,
The silver moon, the little town,
As in the dark I lay me down.

leunig

CONVERT YOUR CAR TO AN ECO-FRIENDLY TOMATO HOTHOUSE ON WHEELS

PUT THAT EMPTY BACK SEAT TO GOOD USE. PLANT A CROP OF TOMATOES.

WEED REGULARLY TO AVOID DRIVING VISIBILITY PROBLEMS.

NETTING MAY BE REQUIRED TO PROTECT YOUR CROP FROM MARAUDING BIRDS AND POSSUMS.

WATER REGULARLY AT THE CAR WASH OR AT THE SERVICE STATION.

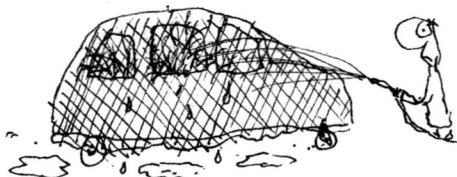

IT WILL ALL PAY OFF WHEN YOU'RE STUCK IN A TRAFFIC JAM AND INSTEAD OF GETTING ANXIOUS YOU JUST LEAN OVER INTO THE BACK SEAT AND CHOMP INTO A BIG PLUMP JUICY RIPE TOMATO.... THE GOOD LIFE.

NEXT YEAR, AVOCADOS, WATER MELONS, PASSION FRUITS. BUT YOU REALLY MUST DO THE WEEDING!

Leunig

I went last night in a driverless car
To a soulless place with a charmless bar
For a tasteless meal with a joyless date;
What a pointless, mindless, useless state.

She said "What a lifeless thing you are!"
So home I went in my driverless car.

Leunig

UNWELL

All the world's great work
is done
Without ambition to excel
By people who proceed
unsung
And feel a little bit
unwell.

In every darkness is a healing joy
In every happiness a disappointment
And in the hopes of every girl and boy
A fly is often in the ointment.

A little fly; a humble tiny life
A wayward, unexpected winged thing
Has introduced all purity to strife
And made the angels weep and laugh and sing.

Leunig

Mr. Curly's Bucket List.

BUCKET 1.
The bucket and spade from his childhood holidays by the sea.

BUCKET 2.
The bucket for watering his pot plants.

BUCKET 3.
The bucket beside his bed when he was sick.

BUCKET 4.
The bucket for milking the goat.

BUCKET 5.
The bucket for bailing water from the boat in rough seas.

BUCKET 6.
The bucket for kitchen scraps.

BUCKET 7.
The bucket for when the roof leaks.

BUCKET 8.
The bucket of beautiful emptiness and perfect peace.

Leunig

I was radicalised
by the butterflies
And later by a tree.
And then a word
from a passing bird
Put radical thoughts
in me.

And I am on the
watch-list now
With the fish and
the pixies too,
Who call to me
with a note of glee
"Just do what
you can do."

Leunig

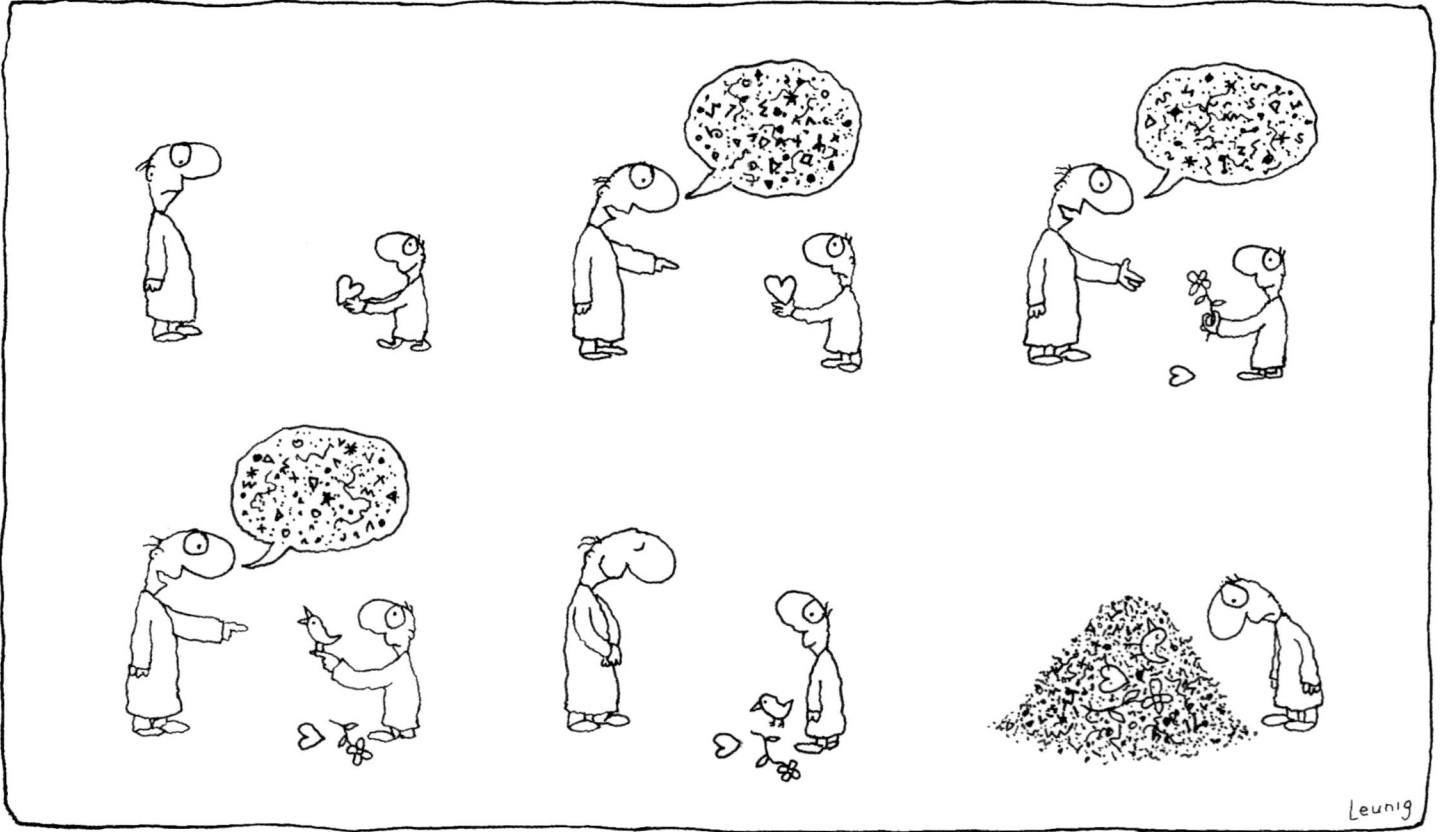

Leunig

Dear Mr. Curly... I'm in Hell at the moment, where an election has just been held. A leader has been returned to power to oversee the booming economy here and supervise the construction of amazing public works and vital infrastructure, so that the people who live in Hell can do Hellish things more easily, more rapidly and more frequently. There is great prosperity and activity here in Hell. and I will be glad to leave this place and return to Curly Flat as soon as possible. Yours truly... with much love from me and the duck.

Vasco Pyjama xx

P.S. Home for Summer!

HELL
PLEASE
SPEED UP

Leunig

SPRING BABY

When Susan Crazy married Brian Mad
What a wild old time they had
During the reception;
Even a conception!

And nine months later little Loopy was born;
A home birth on the neighbour's lawn.
The whole street celebrated.
Her name was hyphenated.

Dear little Loopy Crazy-Mad
Had eyes like her mum and a
smile like her dad.
And just as we had feared;
Her mind was VERY weird.

Leunig

MID-WINTER BLUES

The mid-winter blues
begins in your shoes
Then crawls up your legs
to your knickers
Your heart goes all glum
as the life in your bum
Gets weaker and
everything flickers.

Yet a wee nip of Scotch
and a rain storm to watch
Are pleasures that
carry you through;
Or the gurgling gutter,
some fresh bread and butter
With a warm plate of
old-fashioned stew.

Leunig

Absence makes the heart grow fonder.

Distance makes the feelings wander.

Patience calms the day completely.

Silence makes the bird sing sweetly.

Leunig

Put down your stones... and let those who are without sin among you become radio broadcasters, newspaper columnists or television commentators.

Leunig

CURLYPEDIA

The Australian Parliamentary Choir was established in 1988 to provide an opportunity for members of parliament to sing together in pleasure and goodwill. Since its foundation the choir has not attracted one single member. To keep the idea alive, the Curly Flat Choral Society hold an annual concert on the shores of Lake Lacuna where singers gather together under the name of 'The Choir for the Common Good'. Apart from being lots of fun the concert is in effect a sort of sung prayer for the salvation of the Australian Parliamentary Choir.

Leunig

WE LIVE IN THE BRACE POSITION

Brace position with a tree.

Brace position with other.

Brace position with a garden.

Brace position with a dog.

Leunig

ON A HILL

A man sat quietly on a hill
The moon sat on his head
A friend sat smiling in his heart
The smiling friend was dead.

They spoke together in the dark
Beneath the milky way
And said the words from years ago
That they had failed to say.

A meteor fell gently down
The wise old moon had shone
The stars then sang their words of love
And life continued on.

Leunig

Cinderella could not go to the ball... errr... that is... the Football.

She just couldn't bring herself to do it. She didn't like football one little bit.

Suddenly her fairy godmother arrived and turned a pumpkin into a splendid coach... a football coach!

The coach fell in love with Cinderella and gave up football to be with his sweetheart.

The fairy godmother waved her wand and the coach's footy scarf turned into a vegetable garden.

Then she turned his phone into a chook house full of fine chickens. The coach and Cinderella were very happy. SANITY AT LAST.

Leunig

INTERVIEW WITH AN AUTUMN LEAF.

Q. How do you feel about your forthcoming induction into the Autumn leaf Hall of Fame?

A.L. I feel worn out and blank.

Q. Yes of course, but what do you think about being in the Autumn leaf Hall of Fame?

A.L. I feel nothing really. I don't care. If anything I feel a bit embarrassed and stupid. I don't understand this 'Hall of fame' thing.

Q. But this is a huge honour. You'll be famous. You'll be a legend. Most people would be blown away by such recognition.

A.L. Being blown away is what happens to Autumn leaves anyway, so everything's O.K.

Q. I suppose you're right actually. Autumn leaf, thanks for your time.

A.L. No worries. Thanks for the interview.

Leunig

MOTHERS DAY GIFT IDEAS FOR THOSE WHO HAVE A DIFFICULT AND PAINFUL RELATIONSHIP WITH THEIR MOTHER

A prayer to a candle and a flower.

A few coins to a weary beggar

A song to grandmother moon

Some bread for the birds.

Leunig

THE JOY OF CRAFT BEERS

Craft beers are nothing new to the working class. They are found in situations of domestic prohibition. "WHERE THERE'S A WILL THERE'S A WAY" is the motto.

The advent of beer in cans created new opportunities for craftiness. Concealing a can behind old paint tins in the shed can be an effective ploy.

A classic example of craft beer is a bottle hidden in the wood shed, where it can be consumed quietly, secretly and without any fuss.

The chook house is not so reliable but the ferret cage may safeguard a precious can from snoopers and stickybeaks who are wary of all things weaselly.

YOU WERE A LONG TIME IN THE WOOD SHED BERT...

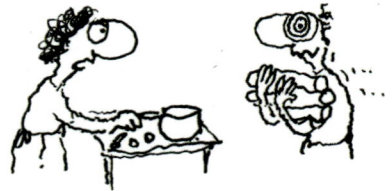

Hiding and imbibing forbidden pleasures on the sly is an ancient craft. Sometimes it is PURE GENIUS

Leunig

VIOLENCE

VIOLINS

Leunig

SUN

Almighty sun, amazing friend,
I praise the blessings that you send:
The morning light, the flowers, the wine,
The playful shadow that is mine,
The crimson cherries in the bowl,
The warmth you bring into the soul.
The paintings on the sky you make,
The silver sparkle on the lake...

And now this wild epiphany:
A melanoma just for me.

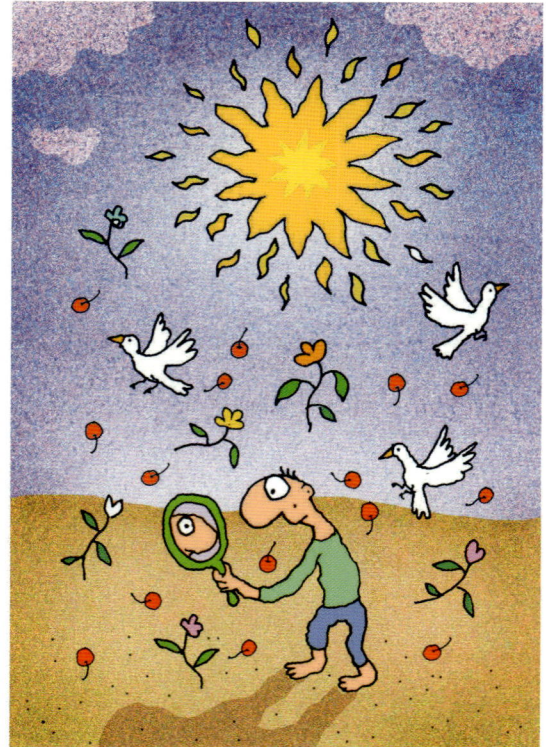

Today is _not_ the International Day of the Cup. No day is.

Without the cup, life would be very difficult. We could live without computers, but not without the cup.

Yet the cup is one of humanity's most important inventions.

Strangely but not surprisingly there is no International Day of the Cup.

It is ancient, universal and timeless. It has no moving parts. It is simple. It is perfect.

The things that matter most in life are not celebrated and win no awards.

Leunig

SPRING

It is Spring.
The world is mad.
The children sing.
The birds are glad.
The flowers grow.
The bees are keen.
The rivers flow
The air is clean
The lass will meet
The joyful lad.
The sun is sweet
The world is mad.

Leunig

IN EVERY BEAST

In every beast there is a man,
In every man there is a boy,
In every boy there is a girl,
In every girl a wild pearl
That grows into a wild tree.

In every tree there is a bird,
In every bird there is a song,
In every song is joy and grief,
In love and life a lovely beast,
In every beast there is a man.

HYMN FOR BED

Oh nest so warm,
Outside the storm
Is dark and cold and grim.
Yet here is grace
And curling space
For love and life and limb.

Oh lovely nest,
You are the best,
You hold me as I cry.
I hope that you
Will see me through
And hold me when I die.

DOG

The news was bad
The day was cold
The world grew sad
As I grew old.

Then as I neared
Catastrophe
A dog appeared
And smiled at me.

It smiled at me
It smiled at ME
A dog came up
And smiled at me!

There he is
The man in high-vis
Holding a sign
They're painting a line
On the road ahead.
His helmet is red
The sign says 'SLOW'
I say hello.
He says g'day
He turns away
He gives a cough
I drive off
Our friendship small
I loved it all
This way of his
The man in high-vis.

Leunig

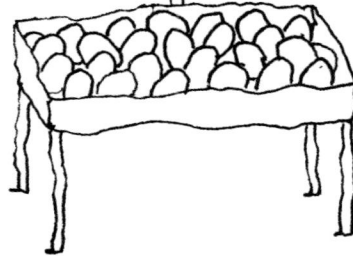

HYMN

Little flower let us pray
The world gets madder every day
There's little I can understand
The anxious hearts, the broken land.

All I want to know is you
Your leaves so green, your petals blue
Your beautiful humility
Are made of love and sanity.

Little flower let us pray
Together in this childish way
For there within your petals curled
Lies wisdom that would heal the world.

Leunig

ODE TO A BOLLARD

How sweet!
Bollards in the street
Such beauty!
Standing there on duty.

I have a favourite one
I think it would be fun
To kiss it.
When I'm at home I miss it.

It's such a sexy bollard.
I am not a dullard
I know that it's the best
It's better than the rest.

I feel so great.
At last I've found a mate.
I thank the stars above.
I think that I'm in love.

Leunig

APOLOGY TO INSECTS

Dear little ant, what have we done to you?
We did not understand the work you do;
The life you bring, the magic you provide,
Instead we sprayed you with insecticide.
We killed the bugs, we killed the land,
We kill the things we do not understand.
We're sorry life has got so sad and sick,
We just don't understand what makes us tick.

Leunig

LIFE'S AMAZING JOURNEY
BETTER
BETTER
WORSE
BETTER
WORSE
BETTER
WORSE
WORSE
BETTER
WORSE
Leunig

RELAXATION EXERCISES FOR THE POLITICALLY AWARE

IN THE STREET.
Bang your head against a lamp post twenty times.

AT WORK
Bang your head against the desk twenty times.

IN THE RESTAURANT
Bang your head into your spaghetti twenty times.

ANYWHERE AND EVERYWHERE
Bang your head against your clenched fists twenty times.

IN YOUR CAR AT THE TRAFFIC LIGHTS.
Toot your horn at the car stopped in front of you twenty times.

With a bit of luck the driver of the car in front of you will get out, come over to your car, grab your head through the open window and bang it against the steering wheel twenty times.

Leunig

GIVE

Give your heart to the outer reaches
Give your mind to the birds
Give your love to peculiar creatures
Give some soul to your words
Give some cheer to the sad old geezers
Give some thanks for the odd.
Give unto Caesar what is Caesar's
But give your art to God.

Leunig

THE LIGHT ON THE HILL

What happened to the light on the hill?

Nobody knows. It's simply not there. It's gone. It fizzled out.

Where is the hill?

The hill has been bulldozed to make way for a freeway.

What did they do with the soil?

They used it for landfill in a wetland where a Casino will be built.

What will the Casino be called?

It will be called 'The Light on the Hill Casino'.

Leunig

PROFILE

I work in a hell hole
I sleep in a tower
I drive through a tunnel
I dream in the shower
I cry in a gridlock
I fall on my face
I cringe in the mirror
I live in disgrace.

Leunig

IT IS

It is, it is,
sang the wonderful bird.
It is what it is
Is the song that I heard.

It is, it is,
said the duck and the fish,
Your life and the world
are not what you wish.

But simply it is,
it's the teapot, the moon,
The song of the bird
and its beautiful tune.

leunig

SOLITUDE

Solitude, a simple den,
A piece of paper and a pen,
A cup of tea, a piece of toast.
A window and the holy ghost.
Some calm, a table and a chair;
The mind is free, the soul is bare,
There's love to make and life to hold.
The ancient tiny thread of gold
That runs through all the joy and gloom
Is found inside this little room.

HE LOST HIS MIND

He lost his mind.
It happened gently.
It felt natural.

He enjoyed his dinner.
He listened to music.
He felt relieved.

It wandered off
on a quiet Saturday
afternoon.

A beautiful sense
of simplicity entered
into him. Before bed
he went outside and
smiled at the stars.

By the time
darkness fell it
had not returned.

Somewhere faraway
in the world his mind
wandered like a happy
old dog, like an autumn
leaf, like a carefree child.

Leunig

SPRING

Spring has come to Curly Flat
The swallow builds her nest of mud
And in her breast the pitter-pat
Of ancient music in her blood.

And in the tiny hearts of bees
The songs of many flowers are sung
As love entwines upon the breeze
With blossoms and the smell of dung.

The soil is ready, warm and willing
All the buds are bursting early
Empty hearts at last are filling
Life is good and sweet and curly.

Leunig

A MOMENT

Life is a donkey. What a surprise!
The trees in the park are graceful and wise.
Love is sanity. Sanity is love.
So sings the blackbird, so said the dove.

Such is the moment. Here is the rain.
Death is a flower. Gone is the pain.
Nothing beneath you, nothing above.
Love is sanity. Sanity is love.

Leunig

THE AWFULISERS

Every night and every day
The awfulisers work away,
Awfulising public places,
Favourite things and little graces;
Awfulising lovely treasures,
Common joys and simple pleasures;
Awfulising far and near
The parts of life we hold so dear:
Democratic, clean and lawful,
Awful, awful, awful, awful.

Leunig

Leunig

THE SYMPTOMS

The death we meet is never late
And never early.
The way ahead is never straight,
It's always curly.

Loveliness is crystal clear
And yet it's pearly.
Far away is very near,
And always curly.

The long forgotten genius within;
The tender innocence beneath the skin,
Living like a pixie in the wild:
The soulful genius of every child
That calls the heart to be alone and rare
And rapturous and rather strange,
and dare
To sing the songs of joy into the land
And say the prayers that none
can understand
To ancestors, the blazing stars at night
Who gave you all this mystery and delight.

Due to climatic conditions, flies are swarming this year. It could be a hell of a summer.

"If you can't beat them, join them" is the catch cry. It is believed that a hybrid 'fluman' would be happier and better suited to the swarming situation of the new world.

But humans too are swarming like never before. The buzzing is deeply frightening.

But so far, the results have been dismal and the worst aspects of both species are coming to the fore.

Flies and humans are so similar that attempts are being made to crossbreed the two species.

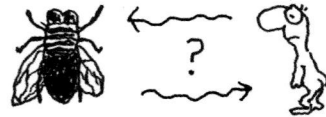

The 'flumans' that have been bred cannot fly and just lie around buzzing. We don't need more of that!

Leunig

UP AND DOWN

I used to watch the sun go down
But now I watch the world go down
I sit and watch the world go down
It hurts to watch the world go down.

I used to see the sun come up
And still I see the sun come up
I wake and watch the sun come up
It's good to see the sun come up.

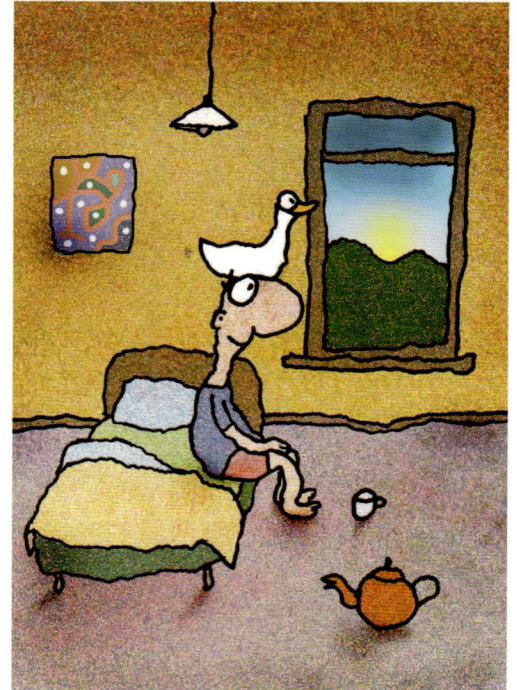

Leunig

THE GLIMMER

You have to wait for the gleam to start,
Patience will not hurt you
Glimmer seeks a weary heart,
Sadness is a virtue.

A cup of tea has been your prayer
And then without a warning,
A tiny sacred speck is there
Gleaming in the morning.

The simple glimmer has arrived,
Life has found a way
All that matters has survived
And love has saved the day.

leunig

JOMO (Joy Of Missing Out.)

Oh the joy of missing out.
When the world begins to shout
And rush towards that shining thing;
The latest bit of mental bling —
Trying to have it, see it, do it,
You simply know you won't go through it;
The anxious clamouring and need
This restless hungry thing to feed.

Instead, you feel the loveliness;
The pleasure of your emptiness.
You spurn the treasure on the shelf
In favour of your peaceful self;
Without regret, without a doubt.
Oh the joy of missing out.

Leunig

THE WALL

"Love in spite of all" it said.
In delicate letters wild and small.
And like a man raised from the dead
He saw the writing on the wall.

Upon this wall that blocked his life
Was scratched a message brief and bare
By an angel with a pocket knife
And genius enough to care.

As grim as any wall could be
A wall of cruelty, shame and dread
It bore the words to set him free
"Love in spite of all" it said.

The Heterosexual Mardi Gras
Is such a plain affair,
A weary dog, an old galah,
An apple and a pear.
A cup of tea, another day
Another joke is made,
Another pile of bills to pay.
Oh what a grand parade.

Leunig

Mary had a little car
Its panels were so bent
That everybody cried hurrah!
Wherever Mary went.
She drove it to the local store
The spectacle was scary
The car was bent a little more
But not as bent as Mary.

Leunig

TO SYBIL

We do it for the common good:
Obedience and submission.
We crawl as we are told we should
Against our intuition.
Except for Sybil, what a girl,
She'll set your heart astir;
Sybil Disobedience,
We'd love some time with her.

Leunig

THE NEW JOURNALISM

PRESS CONFERENCE

Leunig

HOW A DATE FOR CURLY DAY WAS DECIDED UPON.

Curly Day is when the creatures and citizens of Curly Flat celebrate the blessings of their homeland.

Using basic arithmetic and goodwill, possible days were identified and compared, sifted through and averaged out...

The date was settled upon (without squabbling) by establishing a day when the weather would most likely be suitable for a lovely picnic.

... until the most probable and promising day for picnicking and conviviality was decided upon.

Old journals and diaries were studied and good memories were consulted regarding happy picnics and pleasing weather.

Of course it is always understood that things might not turn out as hoped for, in which case the variations and surprises of nature are celebrated with great gusto and good humour.

Leunig

There was a crumpled artist
Who made his crumpled art
From many crumpled feelings
Inside his crumpled heart

He painted crumpled pictures
Of crumpled little flowers
Then crumpled in a crumpled heap
And wept for hours and hours.

Leunig

DANGER
AHEAD.
BEWARE.

HORRIBLE
PEOPLE IN
POSITIONS
OF POWER
AND
INFLUENCE.

Leunig

WINTER

A storm in a tea cup;
a thundery thing.
The rain tumbles down and
the heart starts to sing.
A flicker of lightning,
the sky starts to drop,
The flowers in the vase
do a strange little hop.
The candle flame wobbles,
a tiny bell rings,
My cup runneth over with
beautiful things.

WISH LIST

Sanity, beauty, kindness, care
All so simple if you dare
Sweet forgiveness, patience, peace,
Chickens, blackbirds, ducks and geese.
Trees and flowers, grass and seeds,
Hands and feet and coloured beads.
Cups of tea and distant bells
Clouds and mountains, cooking smells,
A garden path, a wooden chair.
Sanity. beauty. kindness, care.

Leunig

The Curly Flat Festival of Carts

BOYHOOD POEM

I was alone a lot.
I lived a life that I forgot.
I was broken.
I was mended.
I pretended I was loved.
Bits of me were shoved
Against a wall;
The wall I tried to climb
So I could spend some time
With love and joy and you;
The things that every boy
Believes are true.
What is God?
Who am I?
Why is the sky so blue?
Why is the night so black?
Why and who and what?
I was alone a lot.

Leunig

Guests were also served a selection of seasonal canapés including Scottish langoustines wrapped in smoked salmon with citrus crème fraîche, grilled asparagus wrapped in Cumbrian ham, heritage tomato and basil tartare with balsamic pearls and croquettes of confit Windsor lamb. Bowl food included free range chicken with morel mushrooms and young leeks, pea and mint risotto with pea shoots, truffle oil and Parmesan crisps and slow roasted Windsor pork belly with apple compote and crackling. For those with a sweet tooth, there were champagne and pistachio macaroons, orange crème brûlée tartlets and miniature rhubarb crumble tartlets. The food was washed down with Pol Roger Brut Réserve Non Vintage Champagne, and a selection of wines.

Missed out on HARRY AND meghan's wedding Feast but would Be happy with a pie. THANK You.

Leunig

SUMMER

Summer, oh you big hot thing
It's hard to know what you will bring.
Something golden? Something black?
You are such a maniac.

I planted three tomato plants,
I met a dog, we did a dance
Beneath the moon's old silver spell;
It makes tomatoes ripen well.

Or so I used to hear it said
By birds that landed on my head.
And so we dance to welcome back
The great amazing maniac.

Leunig

If we hear the same old dove
Singing in the same old tree
Might this bring us back to love
And beautiful simplicity?

But if we find no sign of these,
Instead, the same old politics,
The babbling celebrities,
A culture made from dirty tricks...

Could we see the same old cat
Sitting in the same old lane
And find some happy truth in that
And know of loveliness again?

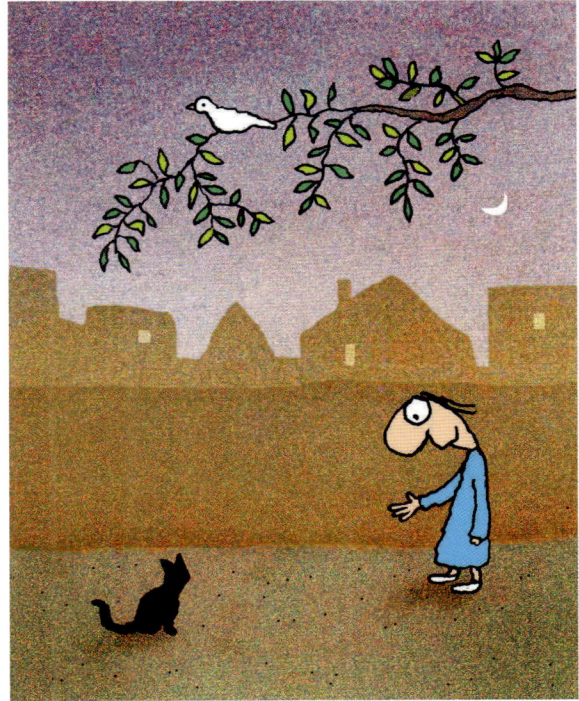

Leunig

It was the worst of times, it was the worst of times. The world was in a terrible ugly mess.

At night many of them stared back at Mother Earth and quietly wept.

People everywhere were treating each other very badly and the mood was unhappy.

On earth women looked up at the distant planet with pain and sorrow in their hearts.

To solve the problems, all males were banished from earth to a distant planet in outer space.

Years passed and the people on both planets grew old and fell silent. For the animals and birds on earth it was the best of times, it was the best of times.

Leunig

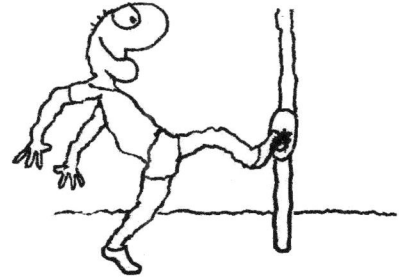

The Puffed-out, Puffed-up Life.

The puffer jacket.

Puffer underpants.

Puffer tablecloth.

The Puffer Flag.

Puffer handkerchief.

Puffer jacket filled with helium.

Leunig

INTRODUCING... *THE CHOLLEY*

For many years, lone supermarket trolleys have been making their way through the streets as they head towards the sea.

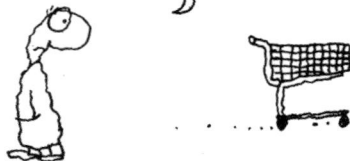

In recent times, lone office chairs have also been seen making eerie journeys through the streets.

Observers confirm that chairs and trolleys have now entered into courtship, mating and breeding-producing a new miracle of evolution and adaptation called the CHOLLEY.

On the right side of history, the cholley may lead the way forward, and be our inspiration as the doomsday clock ticks towards the crossroads of DOOM.

Leunig

The daily news is a sushi train
Stupidity and sex and pain;
Around and round they go repeating,
You just sit there, eating, eating,
Boozing, choosing one more dish;
Murder, madness as you wish,
High school teacher in disgrace!
Latest threat from outer space!
A city bombed, a family slain,
All aboard the sushi train!

Leunig

THE MOOD PIXIES

What is this feeling?
What is this mood you
have woken up with?
This strange atmosphere:
... where did it come from?

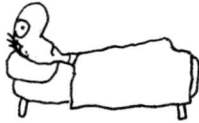

The new day feels a
bit like no other. You
rise and proceed in
wonderment — or
sometimes in discomfort.

Well... while you sleep,
the mood pixies visit
and create a unique
artwork (a mood)
JUST FOR YOU.

It is wise and
profitable to reflect
upon these morning
feelings; this gift
from the mood pixies.

It may not feel right,
but it's what you need.
The mood pixies know
what is required...
Mostly.

But now it's up to
you. What will you
create with this mood
and this new day?
It helps to get up on
the right side of the bed.

Leunig

OLD FASHIONED DO IT YOURSELF DYING.
UNASSISTED TRADITIONAL STYLE.
ALL NATURAL 100% ORGANIC.

Leunig

INNOVATIONS

The road to hell is paved with innovations,
Atom bombs and chemical creations.
The genius of greed goes on forever,
While wickedness is infinitely clever.

But wisdom is the flower needed most
With sanity to be its loving host;
A garden grown for joy and liberation
Made in peace and free from innovation.

Leunig

STAY HOME, STAY SAFE

Fall off a stepladder. Fall down the stairs. Trip on a rug. Trip over the cat.

Have a mishap with the carving knife. Get an electric shock from the toaster. Get bitten by a spider.

Burn yourself with hot oil. Have an accident with a power tool. Crush your fingers in the door.

Destroy your mind in front of a screen. Report your neighbours to the police for being human. Go around the twist. Go up the wall.

STAY HOME. GOOD LUCK   Leunig

THE CANCELLED MAN

He was CANCELLED, shamed, outed, condemned, disgraced and named. His life was DESTROYED.

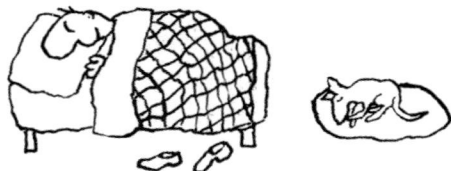

It was an old friend who told him that his life had been ruined. The friend told him he looked remarkably well in spite of this hideous disaster.

Yet strangely he knew nothing of all this. While it was happening he was sleeping, walking in the forest, collecting sea shells, painting pictures and listening to the songs of birds in his garden.

That night the cancelled man saw a shooting star and he made a wish. He wished for warm sunny weather so that his tomatoes would ripen well.

Leunig